Do you Know

Shitty People

The vulgar and Delightful Adult Coloring Book

By

S.B. Nozaz

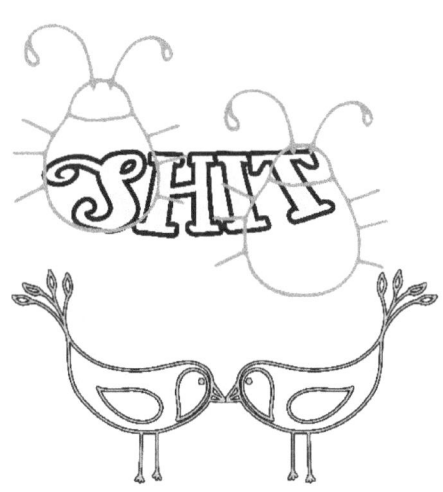

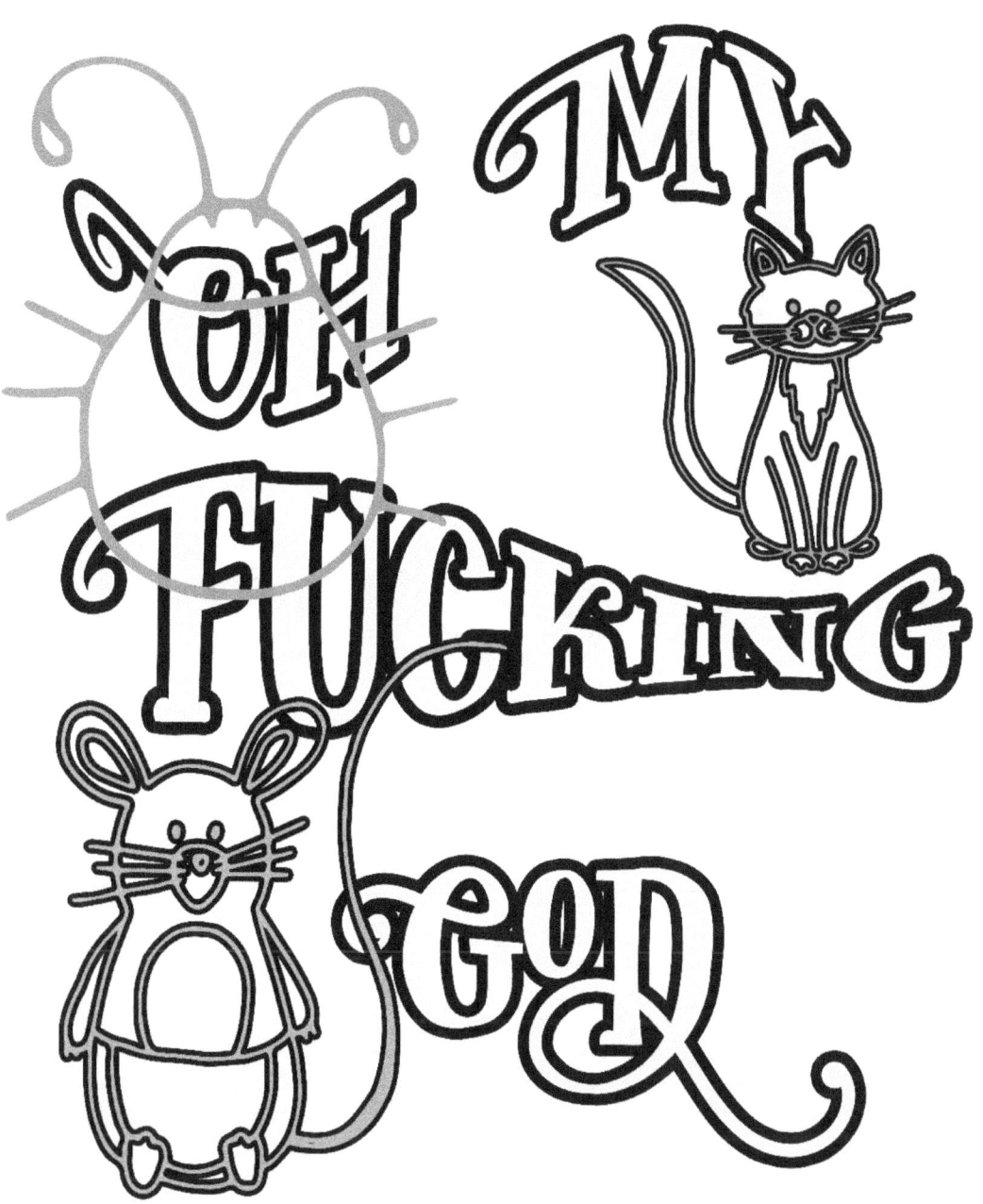

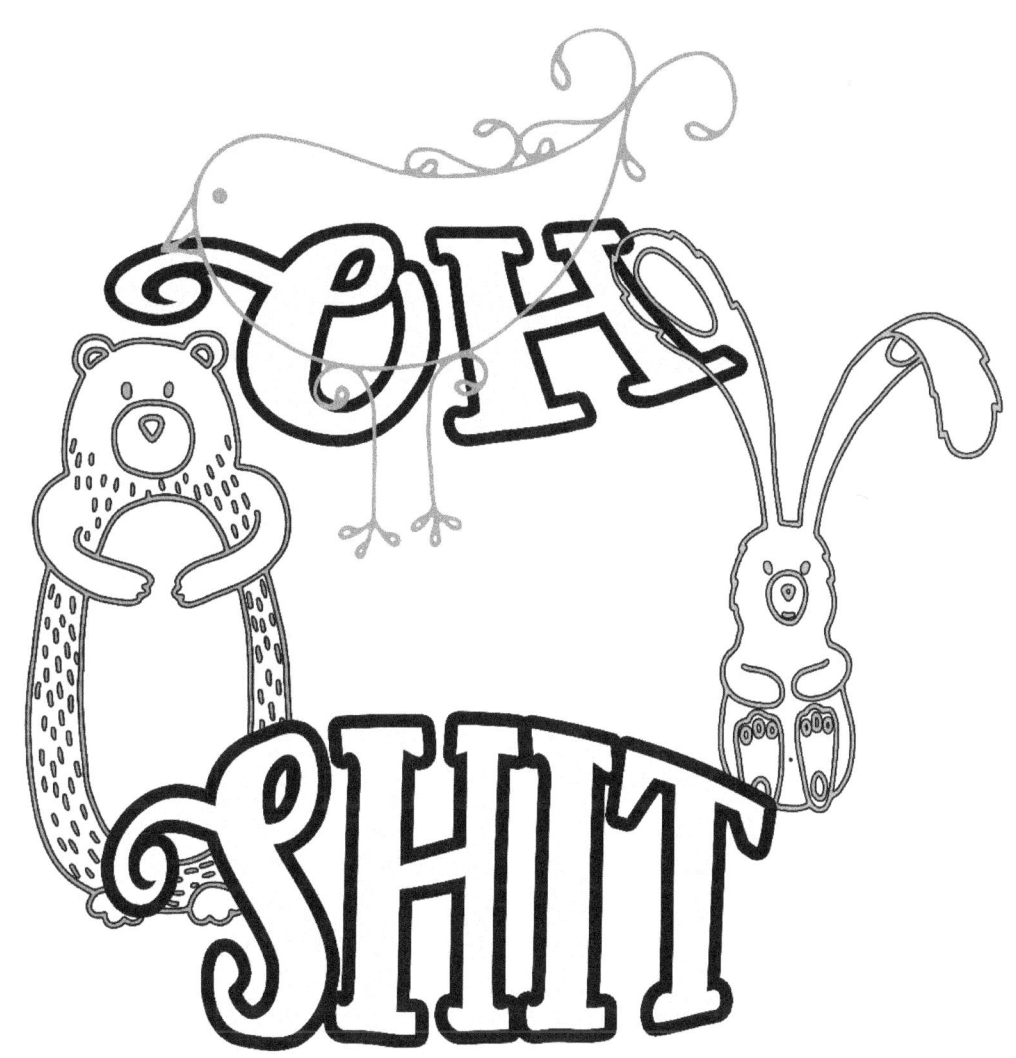

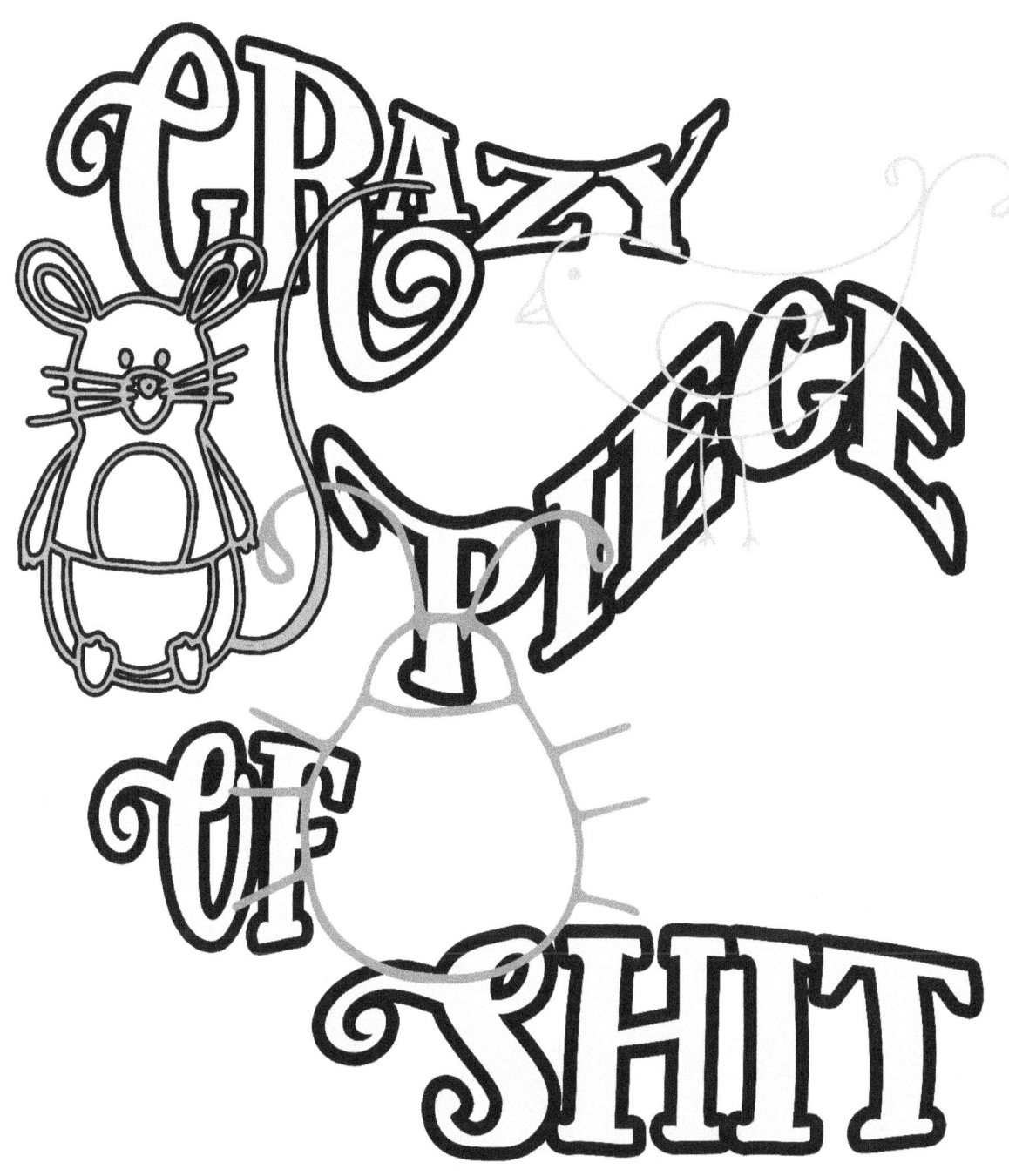

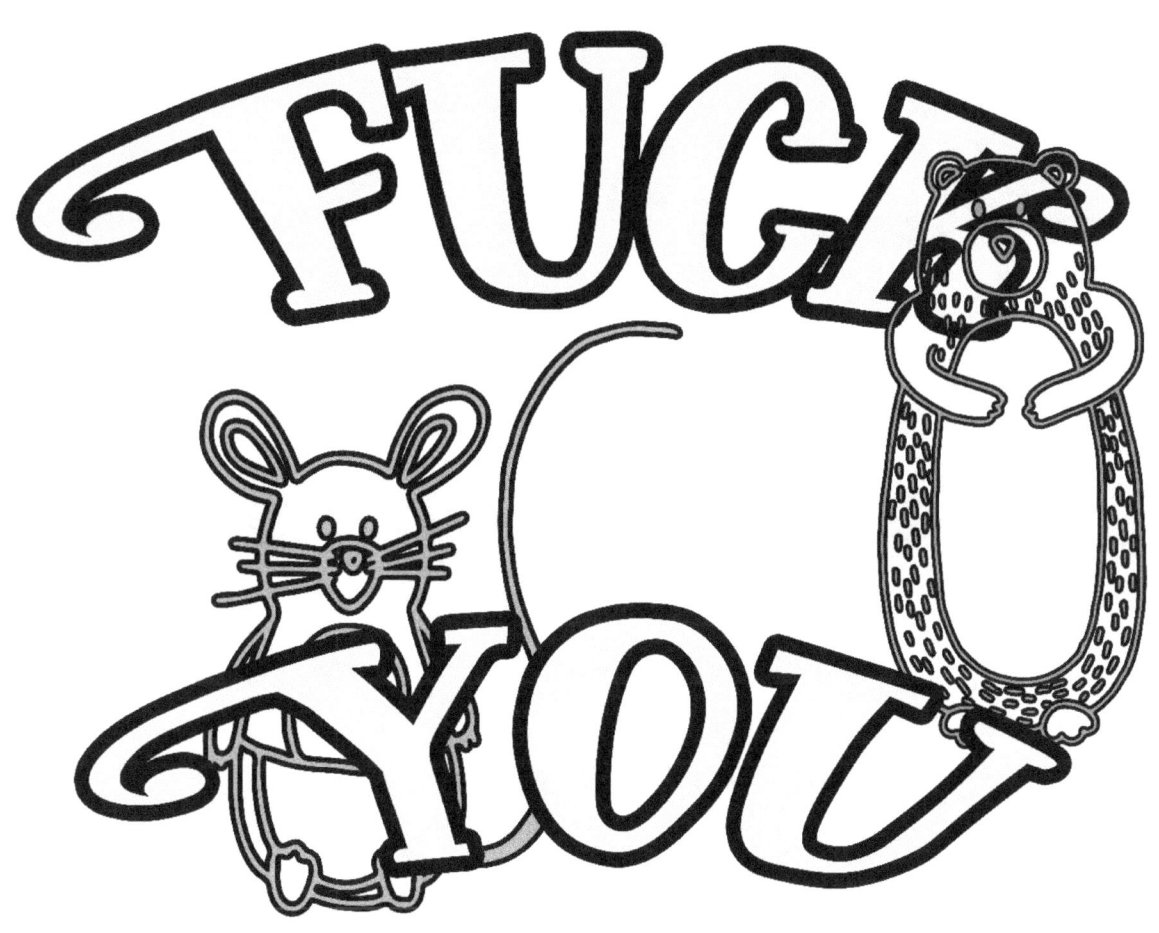

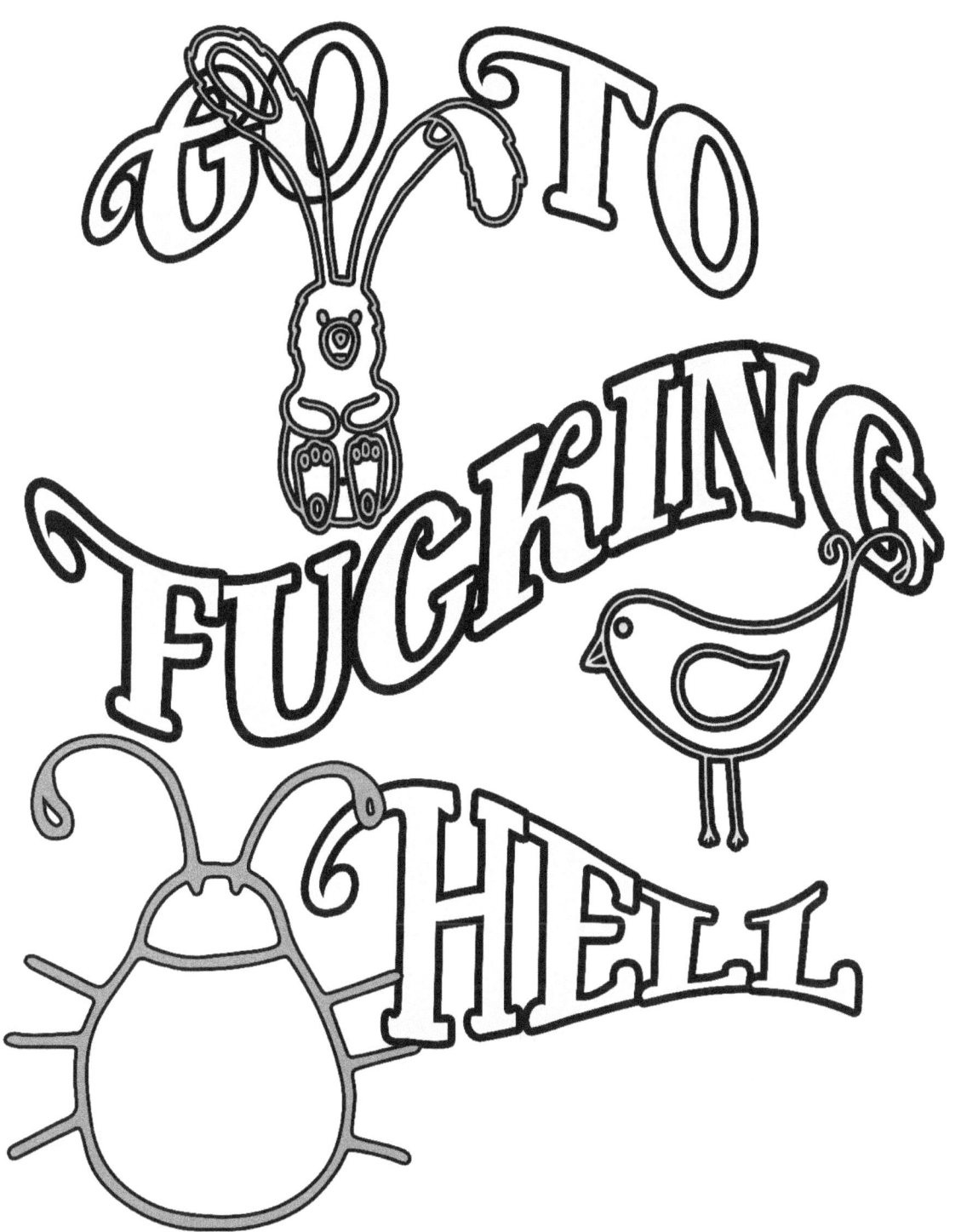

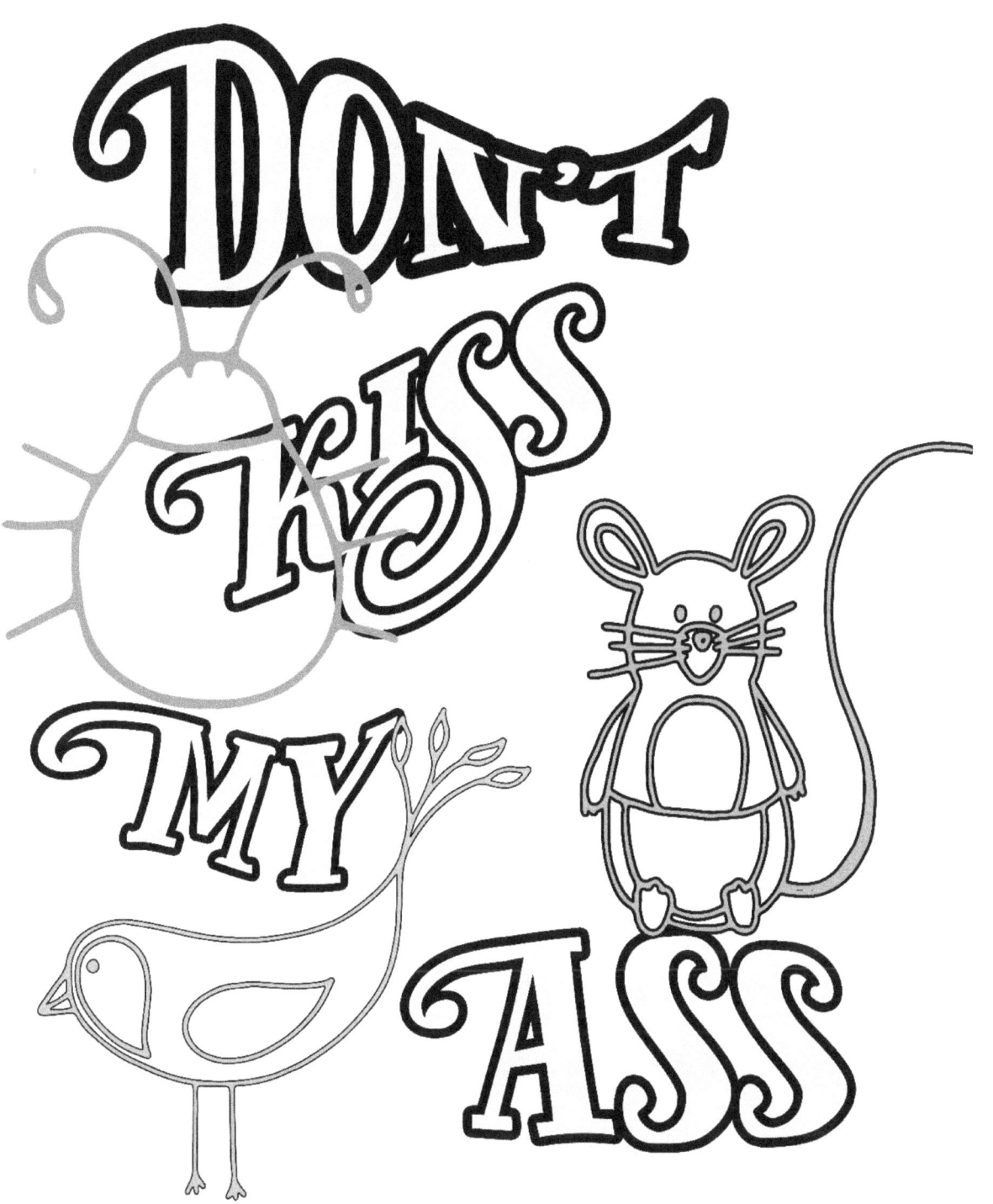

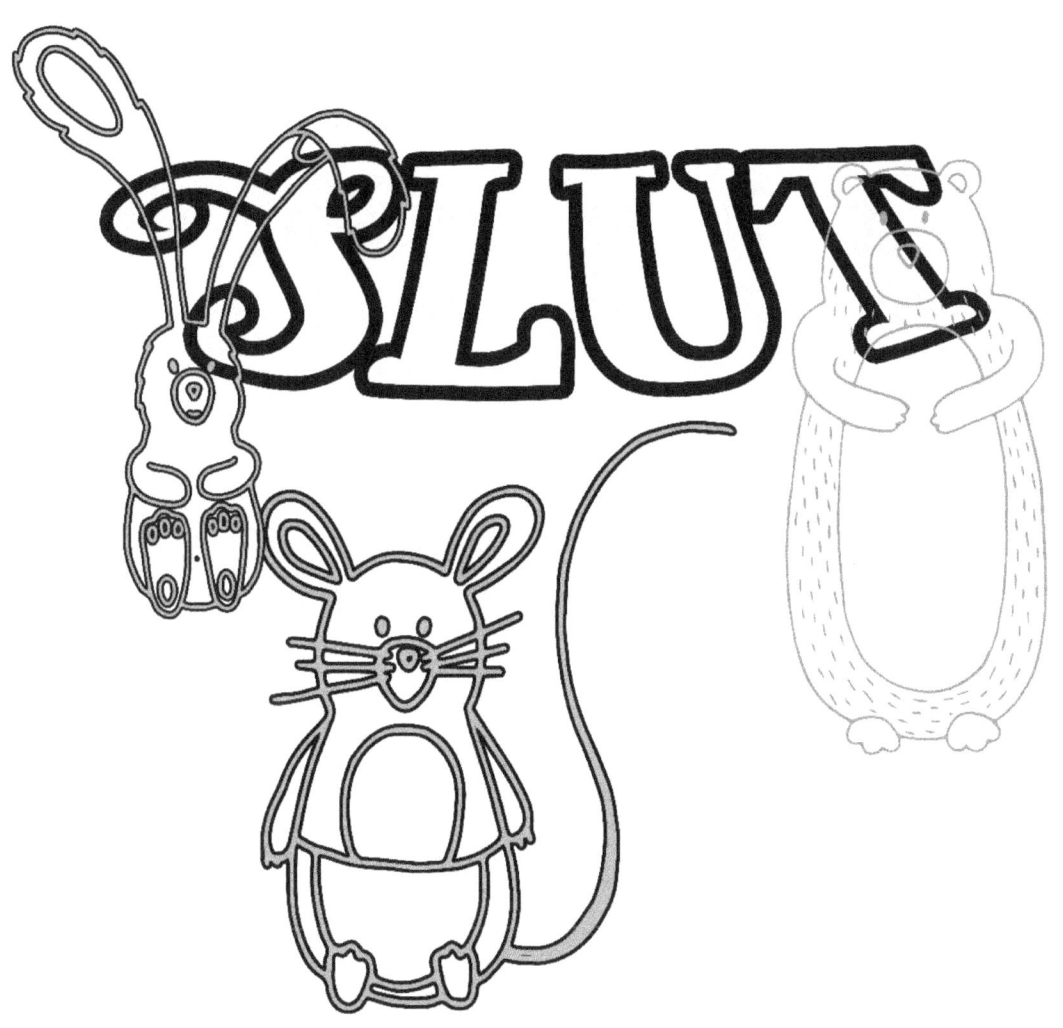

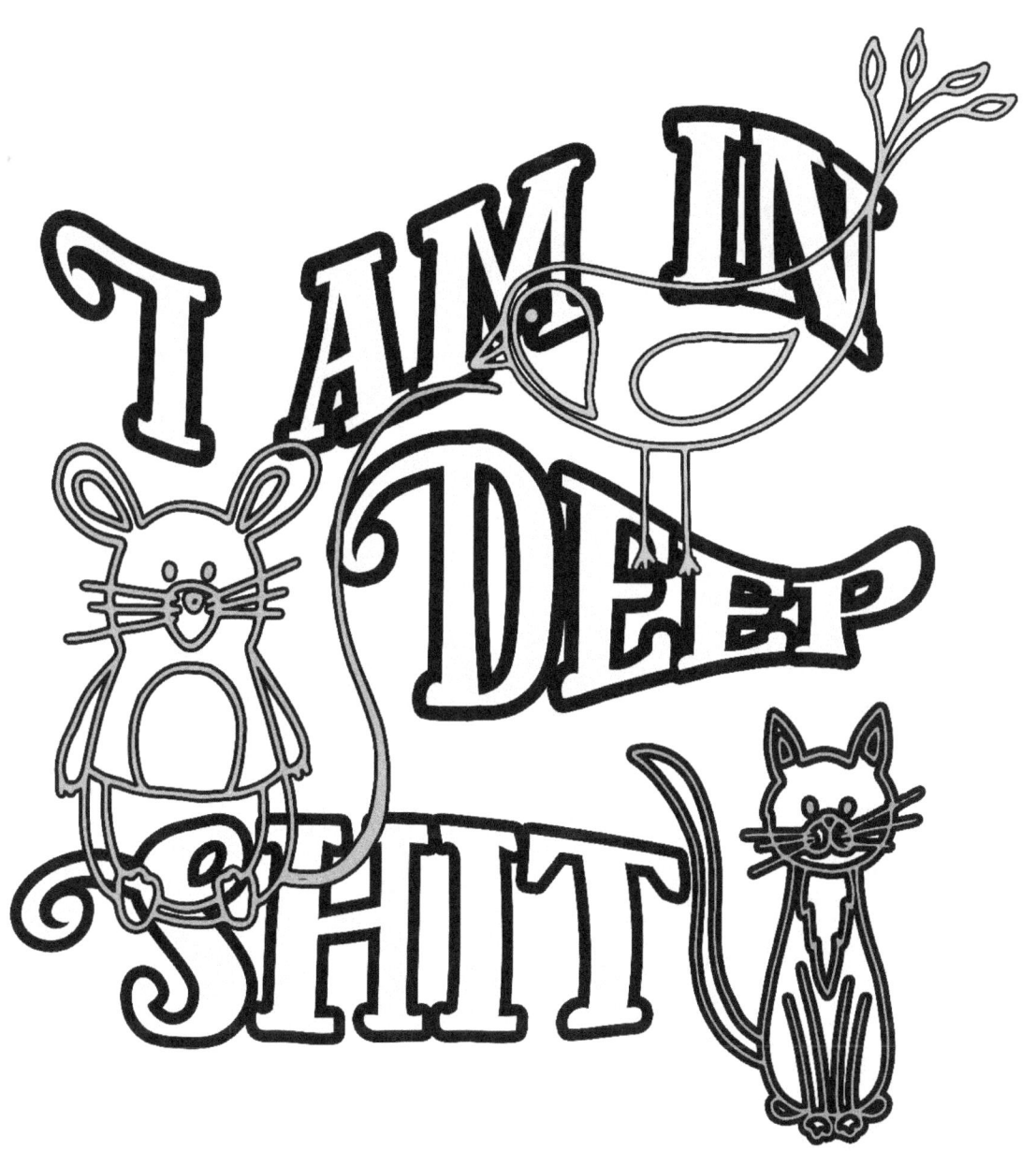

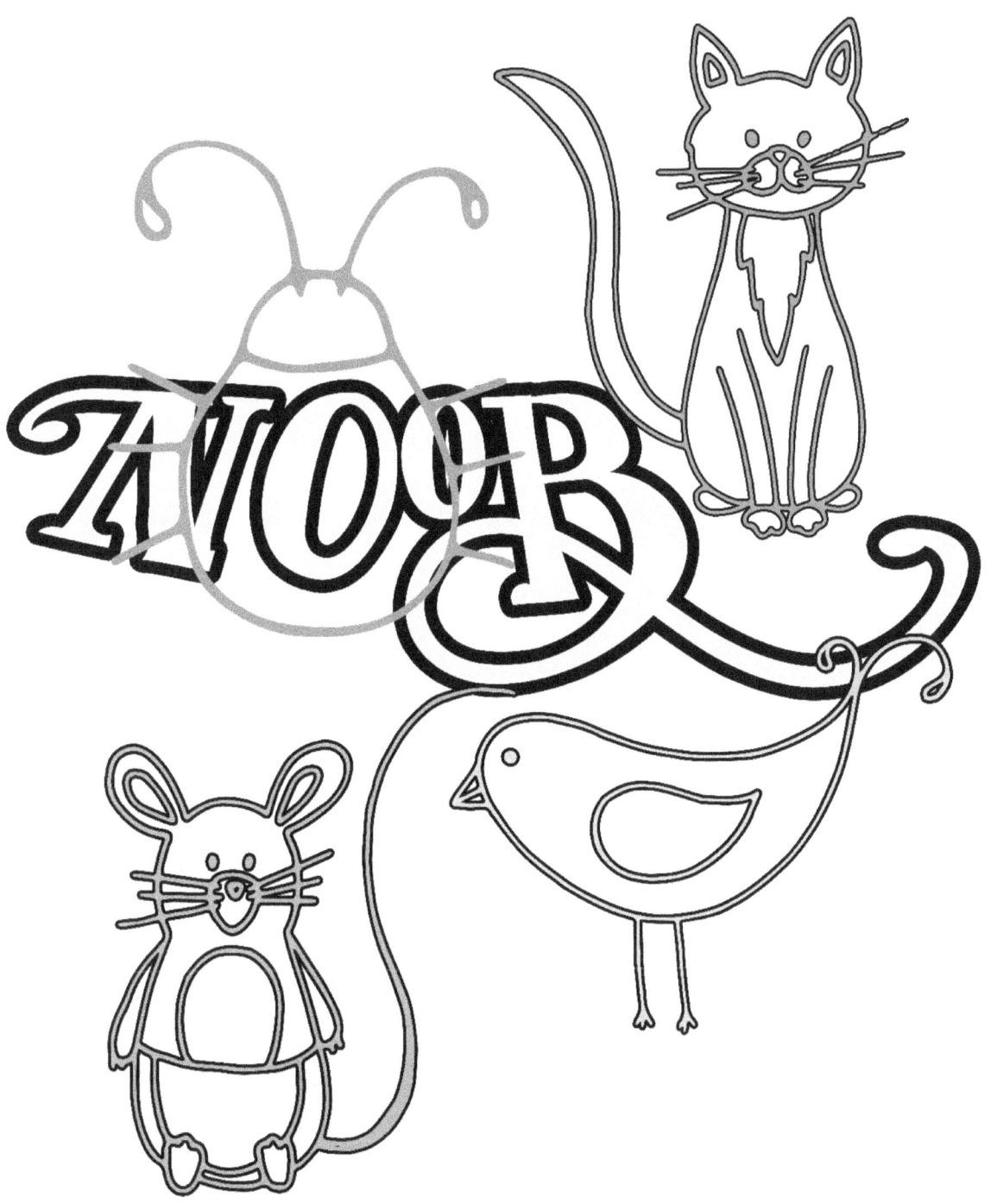

GO JERK YOURSELF

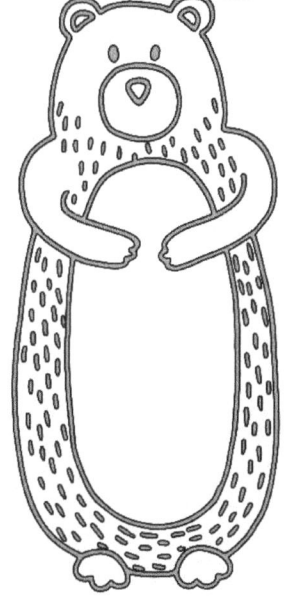

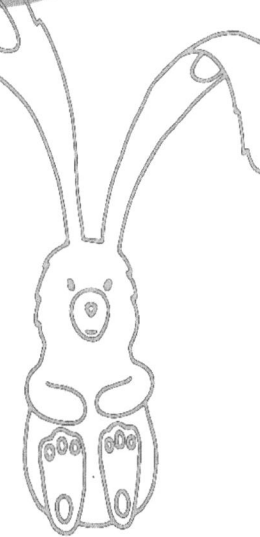

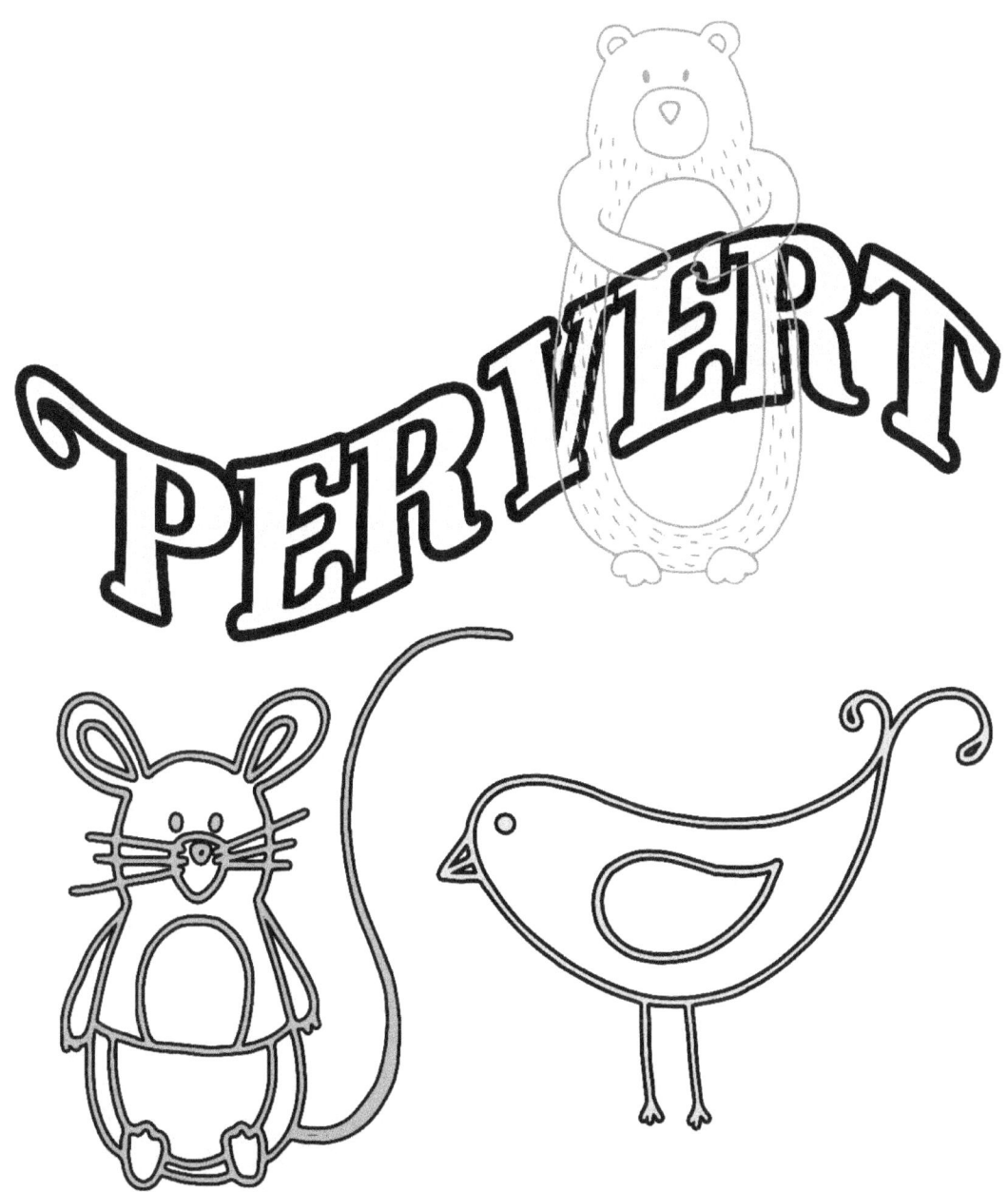

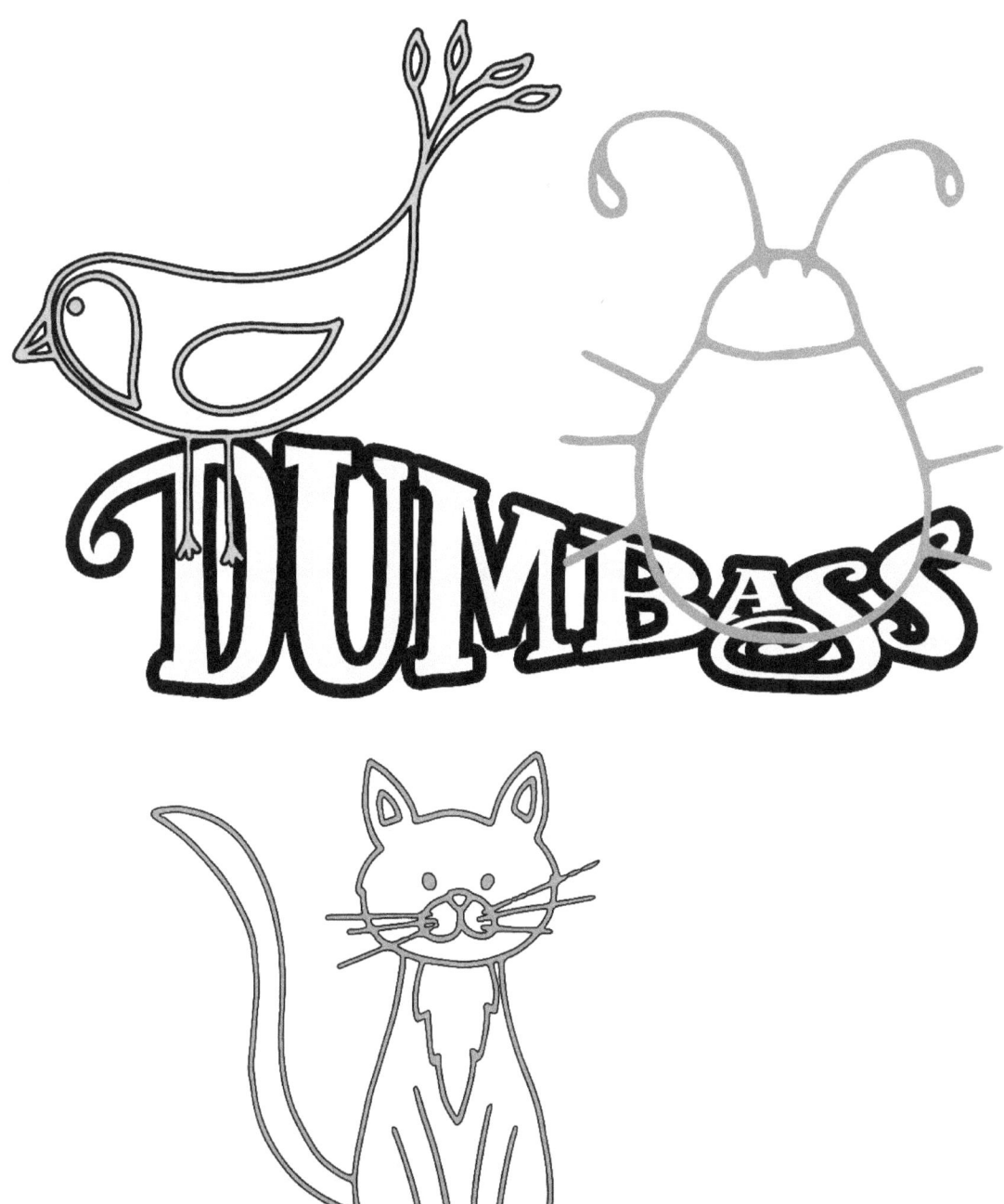

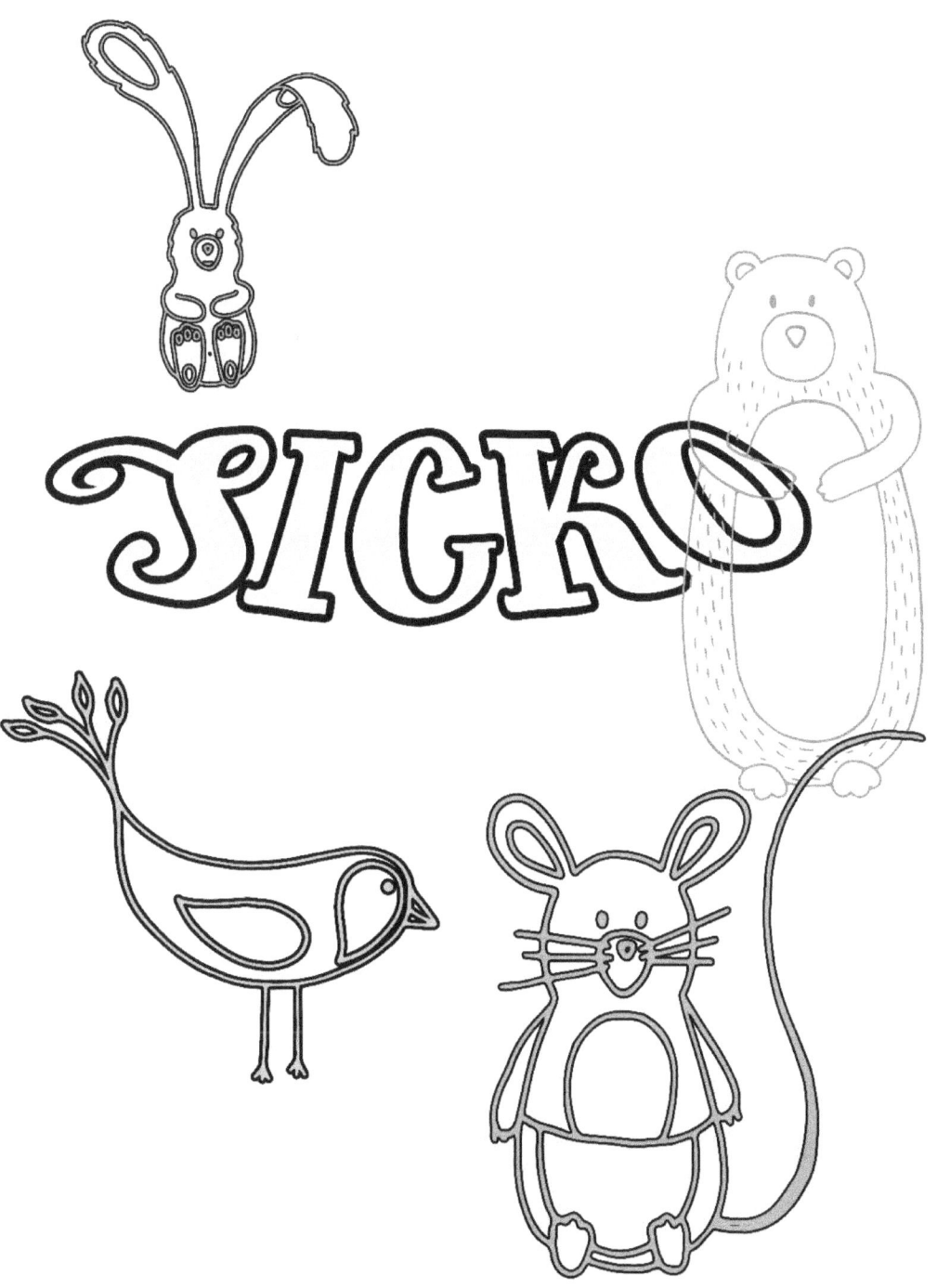

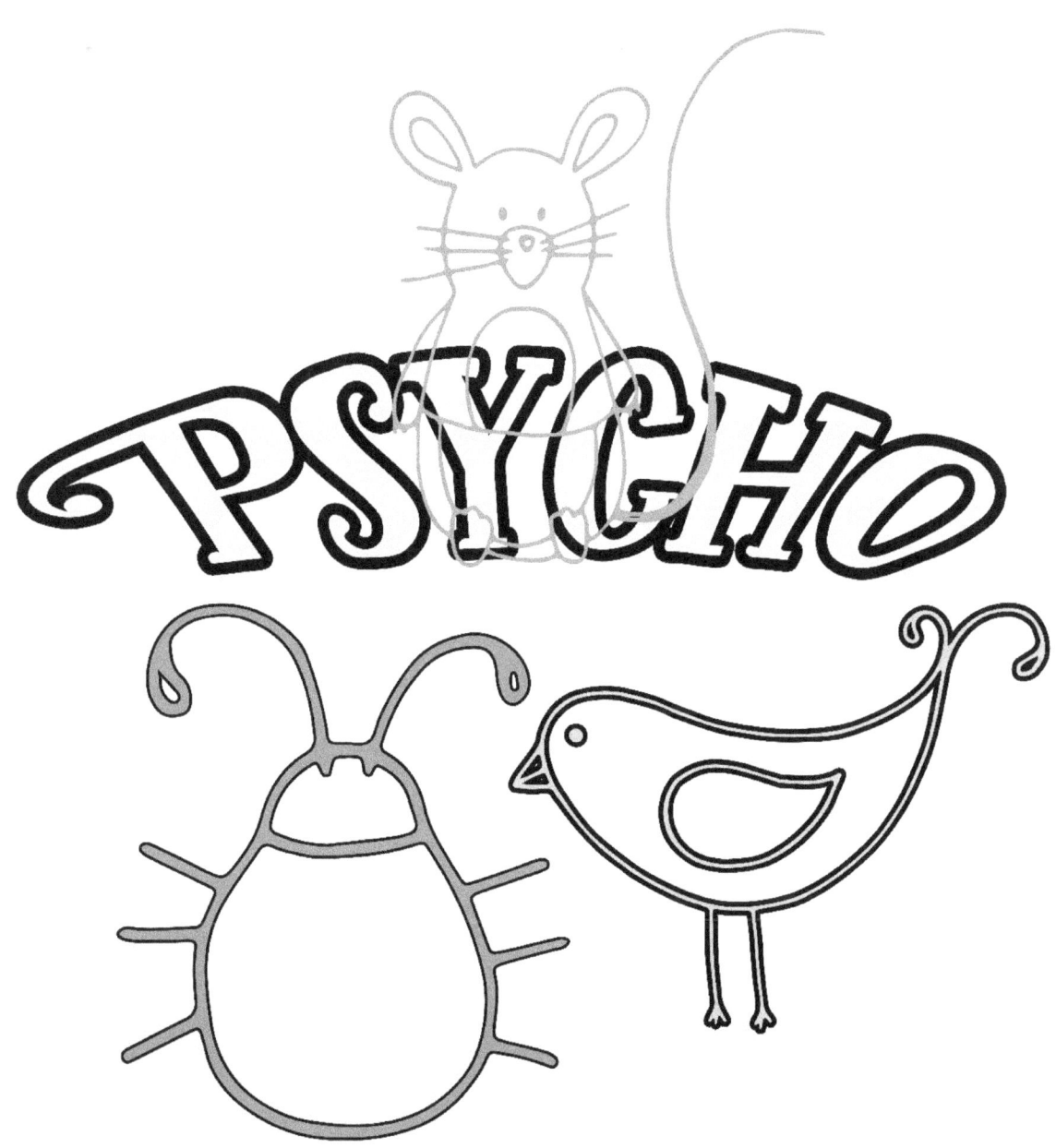

IDIOT

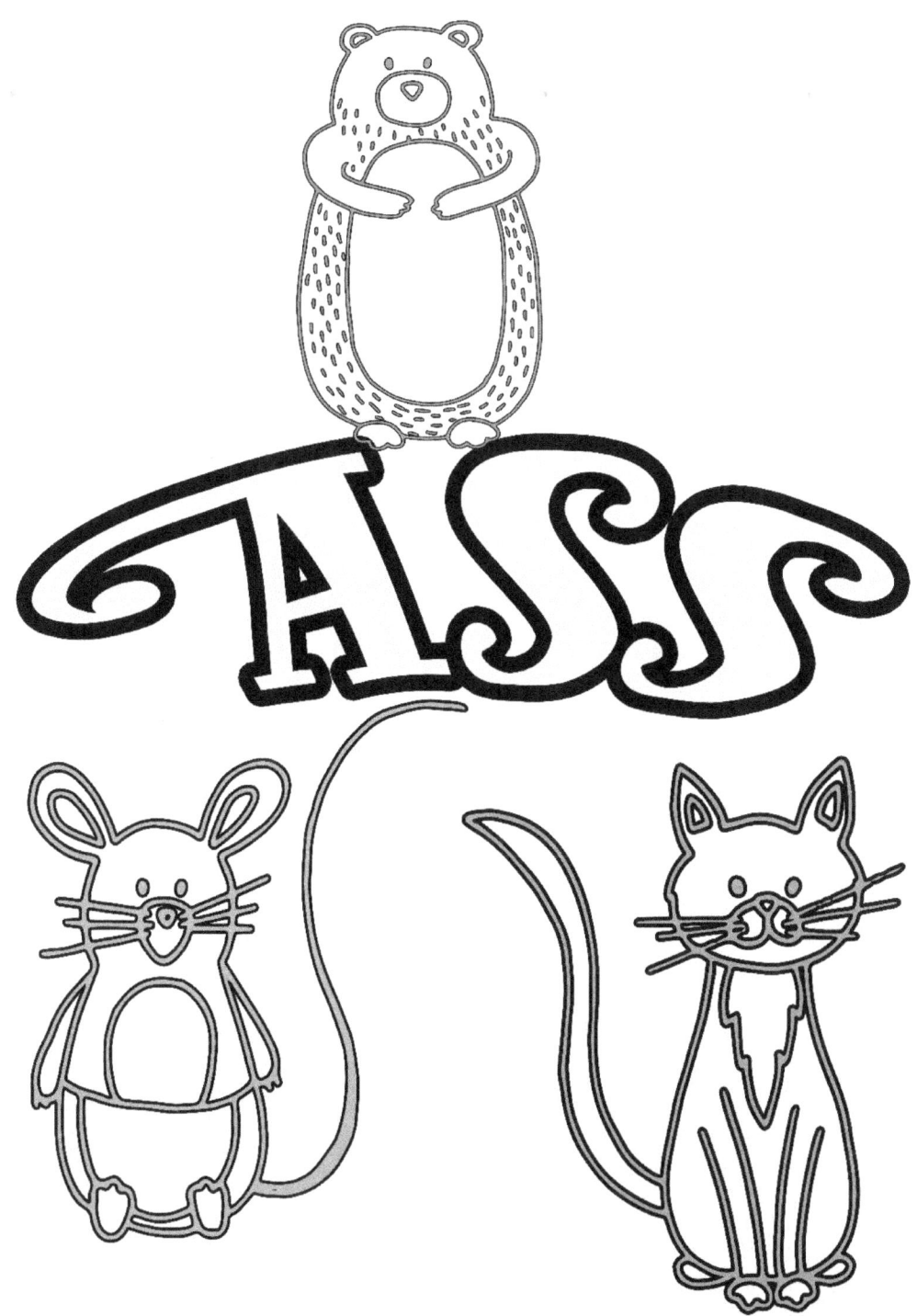

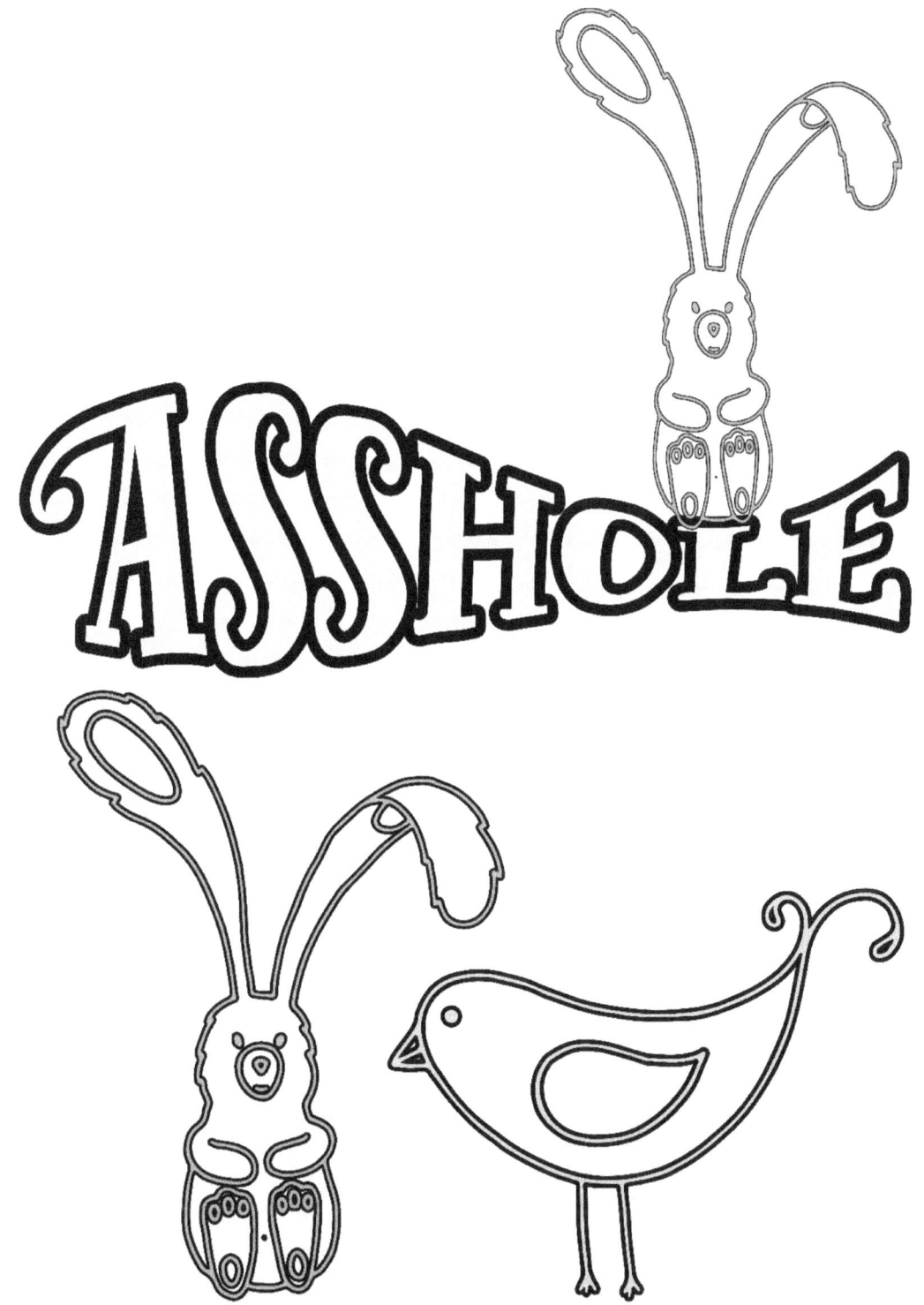

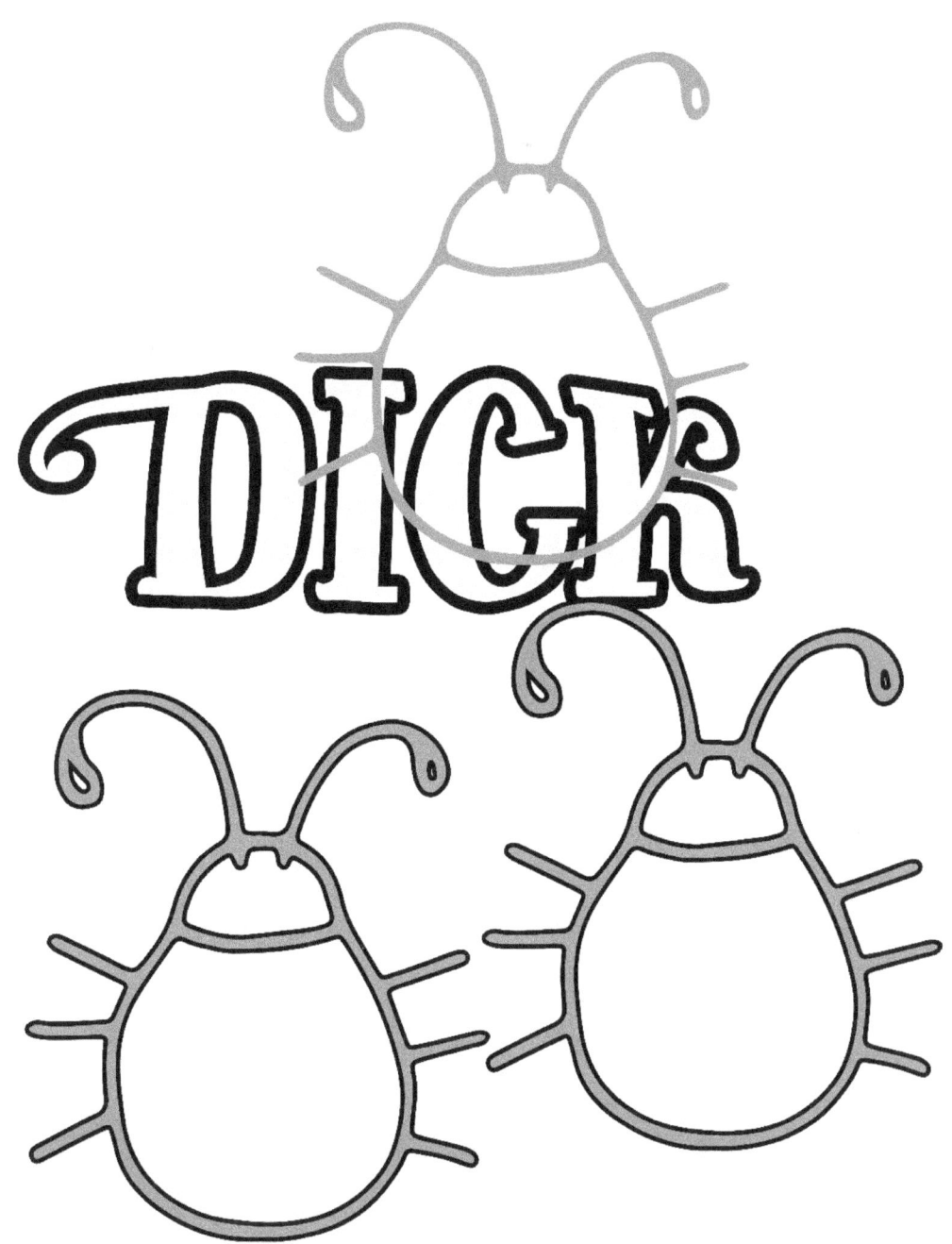

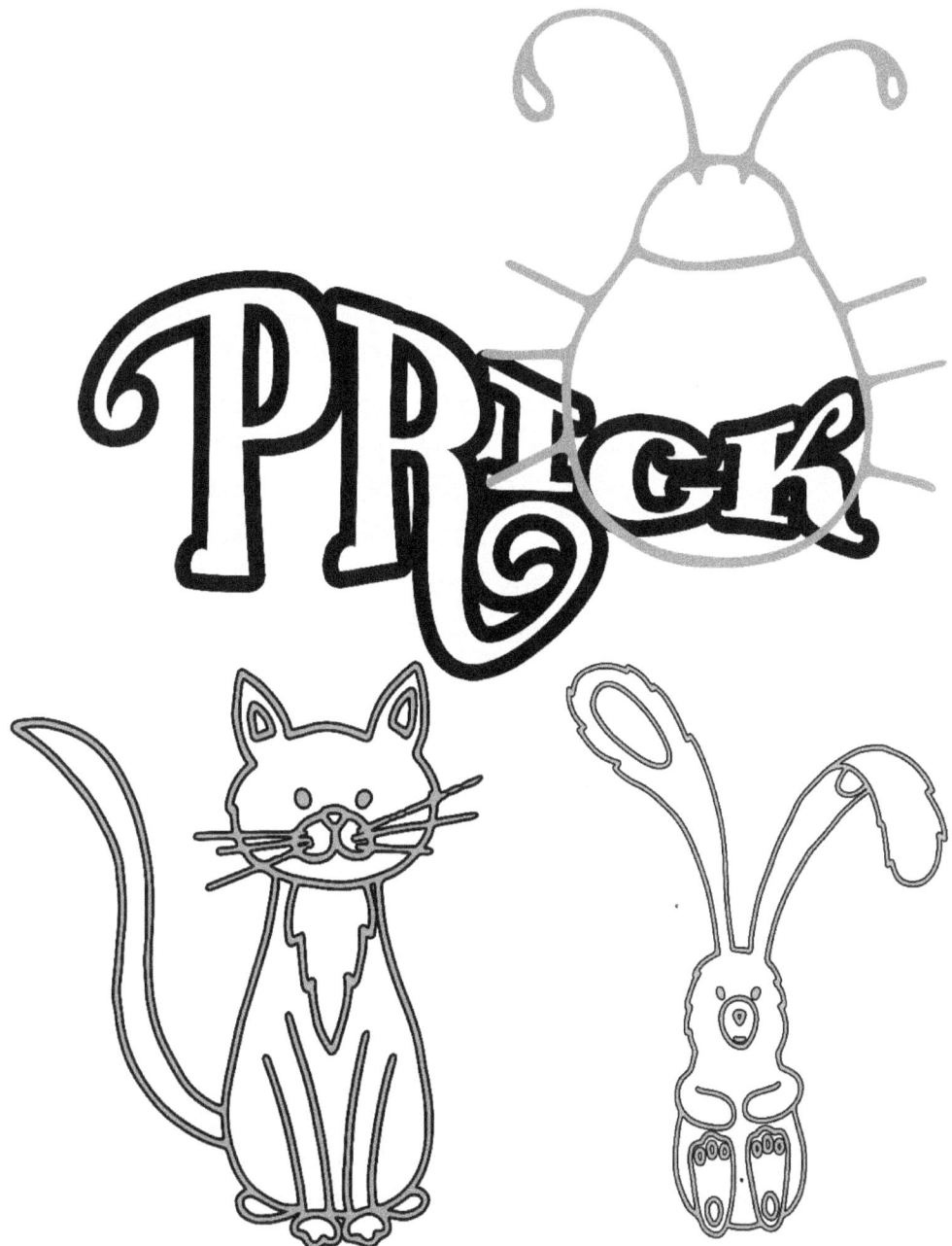

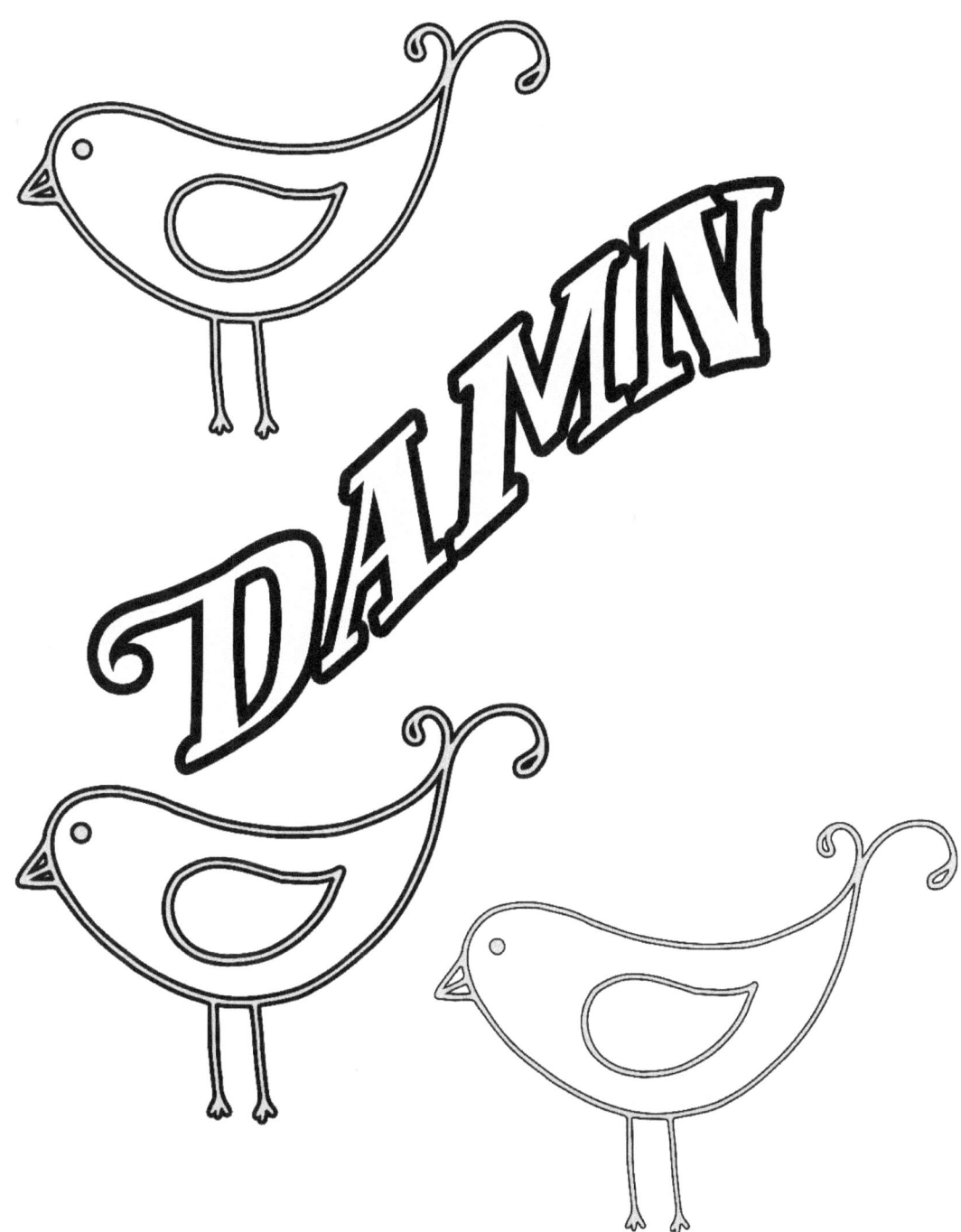

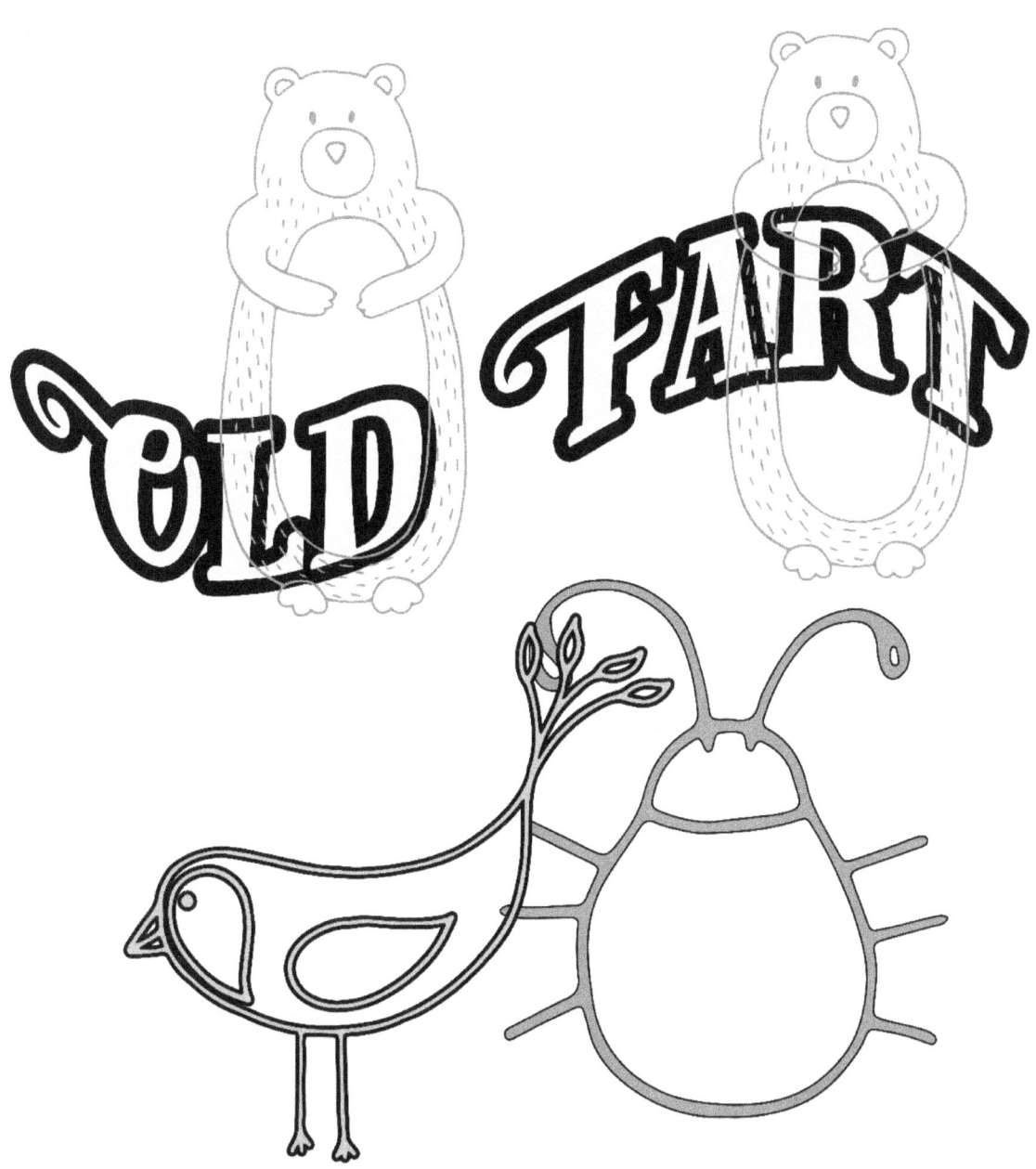

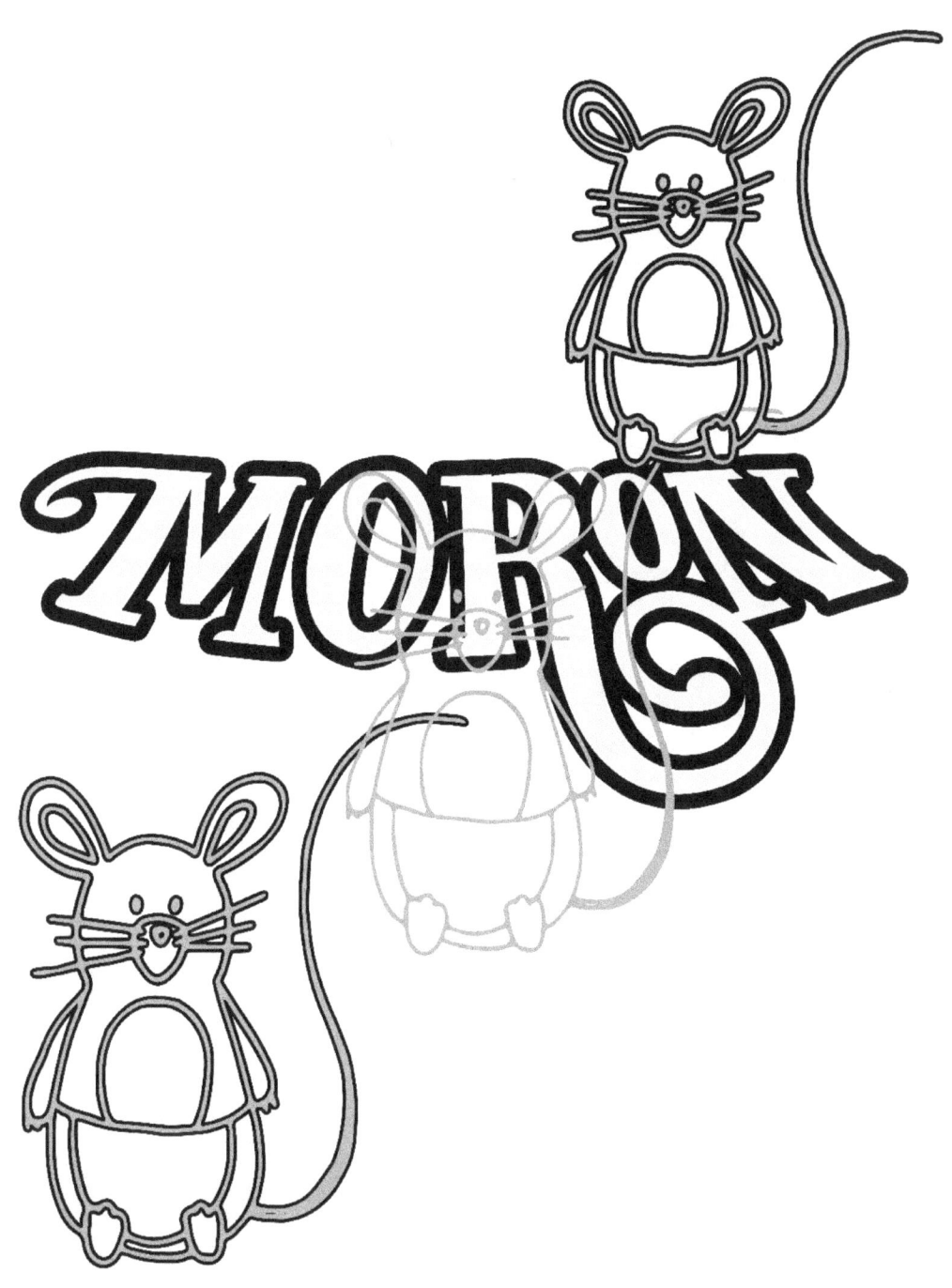

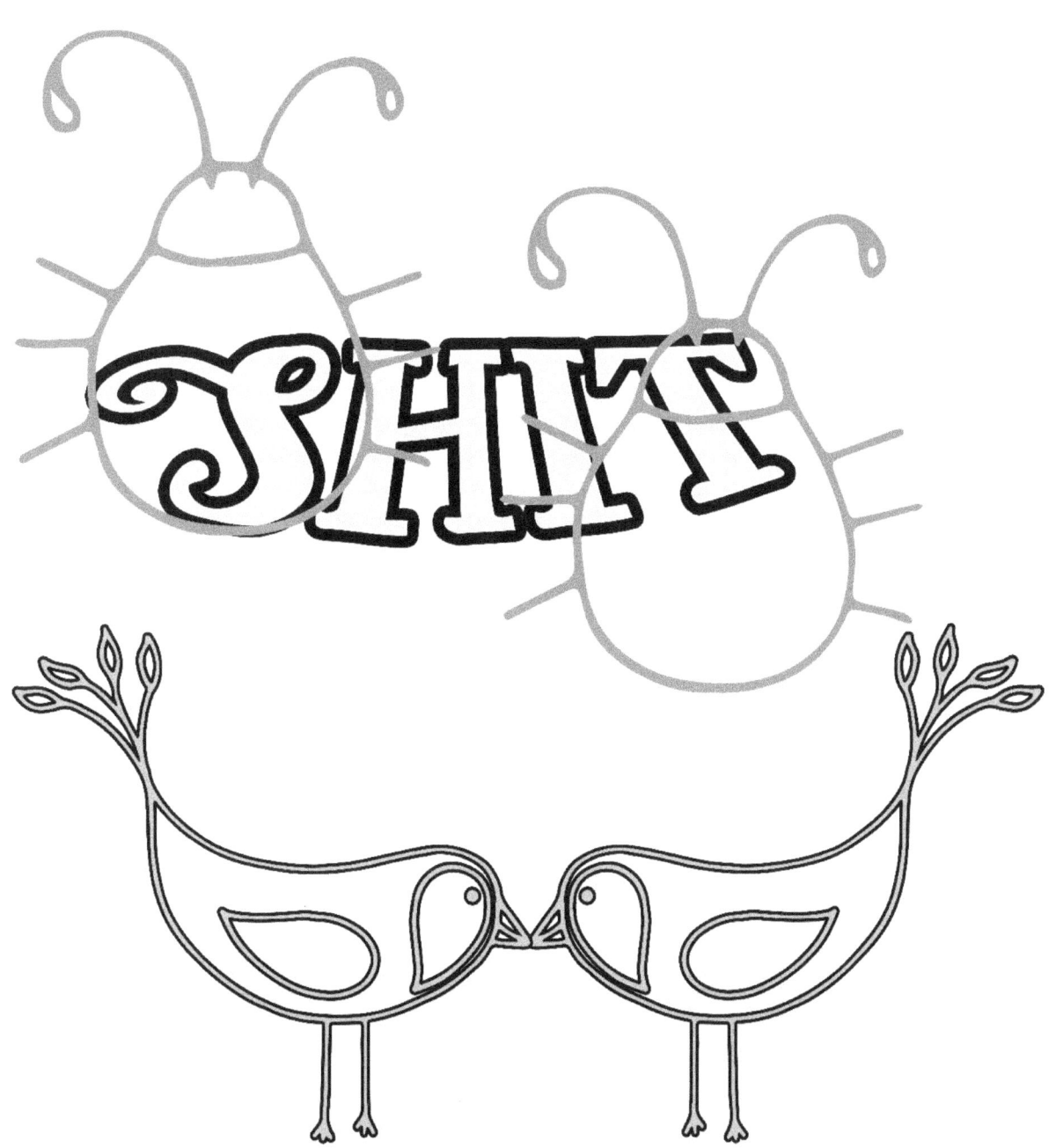

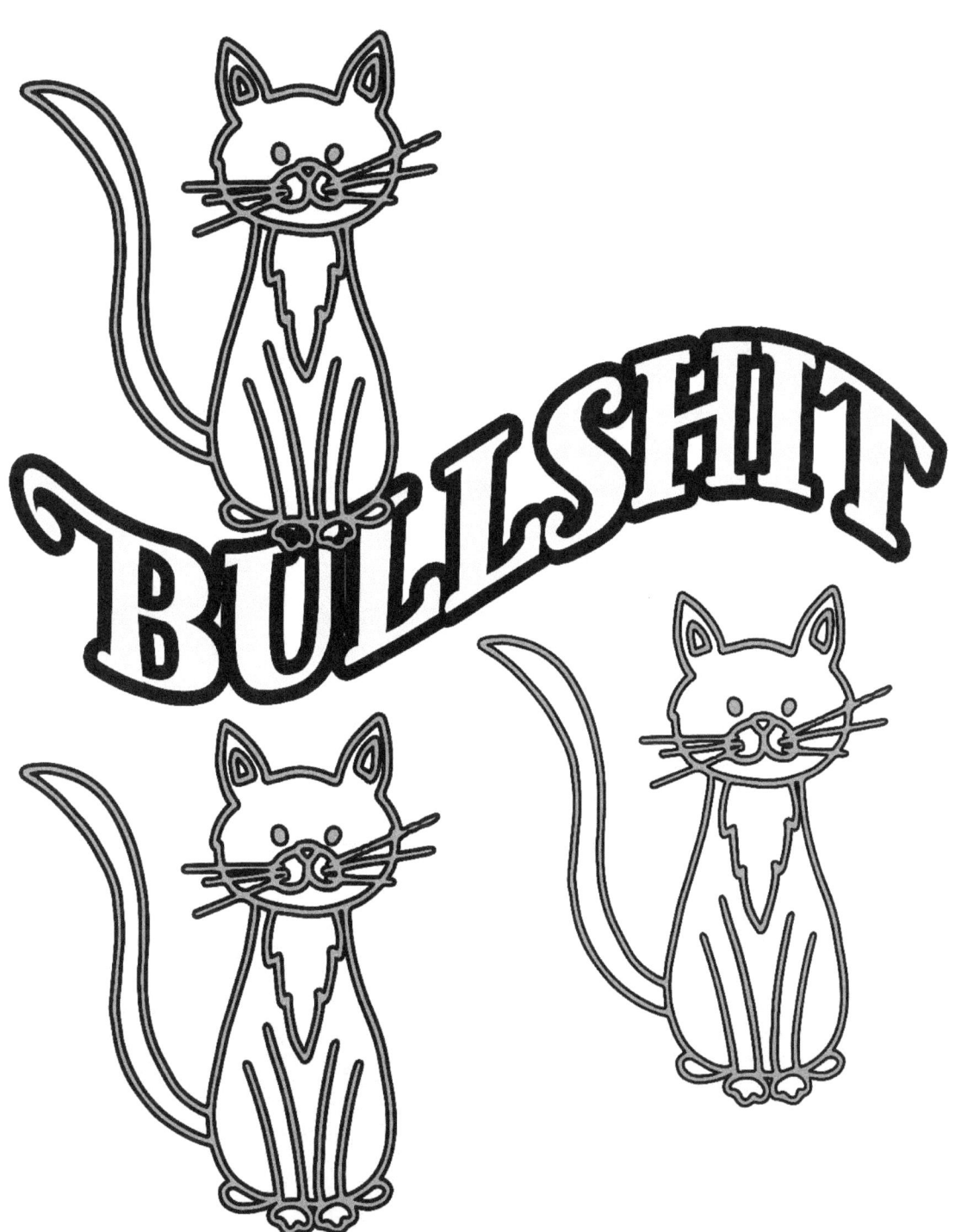

Note

www.ingramcontent.com/pod-product-compliance
Lightning Source LLC
Chambersburg PA
CBHW080638190526
45169CB00009B/3421